little book of

Alcohol-free
Cocktails

hamlyn

First published in 2001 by Hamlyn,
a division of Octopus Publishing Group Limited
2–4 Heron Quays, London E14 4JP

British Library Cataloguing-in-Publication Data
A catalogue record for this book is available from the British Library

ISBN 0 600 60435 7

Printed in China

Notes for American readers

The measure that has been used in the recipes is based on a bar measure,
which is 25 ml (1 fl oz). If preferred, a different volume can be used
providing the proportions are kept constant within a drink and suitable
adjustments are made to spoon measurements, where they occur.

Standard level spoon measurements are used in all recipes.
1 tablespoon = one 15 ml spoon
1 teaspoon = one 5 ml spoon
Imperial and metric measurements have been given in some of the recipes.
Use one set of measurements only.

UK	US
caster sugar	granulated sugar
cocktail cherries	maraschino cherries
cocktail stick	toothpick
double cream	heavy cream
drinking chocolate	presweetened cocoa powder
icing sugar	confectioners' sugar
jug	pitcher
lemon rind	lemon peel or zest
single cream	light cream
soda water	club soda

SAFETY NOTE The Department of Health advises that eggs should not be
consumed raw. This book contains recipes made with raw eggs. It is prudent
for more vulnerable people such as pregnant and nursing mothers, invalids,
the elderly, babies and young children to avoid these recipes.

Contents

CATERING FOR CROWDS 8
This chapter contains a wide-ranging selection of delicious drinks for large numbers of people. Choose from Tropical Treat, an unusual fresh pineapple drink with a yogurt base, the refreshing Grapefruit Mint Cooler, or the fruity Midsummer Punch.

FRUIT AND VEGETABLES 34
Romanov Fizz and Bugs Bunny are among the many drinks in the chapter that will appeal as much to health-conscious adults as to children.

ROUND THE CLOCK 64
Iced Apple Tea and Florentine Coffee can be enjoyed at any time of the day, while more sophisticated cocktails such as Pink Tonic and Virgin Mary will appeal to those who prefer something more in the style of an alcoholic drink at cocktail hour.

Introduction

Alcohol-free drinks are becoming increasingly popular with those who are driving, those who worry about their health, those who simply prefer not to drink, and with children who want sophisticated drinks of their own. At parties it is essential to provide a range of soft drinks, so why not make your guests feel especially welcome, whether they are drinking or not, by providing a range of both alcoholic and alcohol-free cocktails. Long gone are the days when a few bottles of cola were considered sufficient for the non-drinkers.

Just because cocktails contain no alcohol doesn't mean they have to be dull and predictable. This book offers a selection of tempting drinks for any occasion, whether it is a summer garden party, a New Year's gathering or a dinner party.

By the use of unusual ingredients and exciting combinations, alcohol-free drinks can be just as appealing as those with alcohol.

When making alcohol-free drinks, use the best quality ingredients for the best results. This is especially important with fruit- and vegetable-based drinks as the quality of the fresh produce will have a great effect on the flavour of the finished drink. Choose ripe, juicy fruits, but avoid those that are over-ripe or too soft as the flavour will be affected. An electric juicer is a useful tool for those who plan to make a lot of fruit-based drinks, as it allows you to produce your own delicious juices from all sorts of fruits. Homemade juice is more flavoursome and certainly contains more nutrients than bought juices, and you will be able to make just about any own exciting ideas.

One of the keys to making alcohol-free drinks seem special is in their presentation. Invest a bit of time and effort choosing the right glasses and making decorations for the drinks; they can be prepared in advance, leaving you time to relax when your guests arrive.

Many fruits lend themselves to decorating the rims of glasses. Try fixing slices of lemon, orange, lime, kiwifruit, apple or starfruit over the rim, or cut wedges of pineapple, mango, banana or melon and slide these in place. Alternatively, spear them on cocktail sticks and suspend them over the drink.

For a special occasion, consider frosting the rims of the glasses. This can be done with sugar or salt, depending on the drink. Usually the rim of the glass is dipped in beaten egg white, then in the salt or sugar, but it is possible to dip the rim in a syrup such as grenadine, then in the sugar. Glasses can also be filmed with Angostura bitters; although alcoholic, the bitters are used in such small quantities that the alcohol content is negligible.

Although most of the drinks in this book are suitable for special occasions, many are simple enough to become everyday favourites. And some of the drinks, especially those based on fruit juices, are packed with nutrients and offer a great way to provide children with their necessary vitamins.

Sugar Syrup
This may be used instead of sugar to sweeten cocktails and give them more body. It can be bought, but is simple to make. Put 4 tablespoons of caster sugar and 4 tablespoons of water in a small pan and stir over a low heat until the sugar has dissolved. Bring to the boil and boil, without stirring, for 1–2 minutes. It can be stored in a sterilized bottle in the refrigerator for up to 2 months.

Catering for Crowds

Cool Passion

500 ml (17 fl oz) orange
   and passion fruit juice
1 litre (1¾ pints)
   pineapple juice
1.5 litres (2½ pints)
   lemonade
crushed ice

to decorate
blackberries
mint sprigs

Pour the two fruit juices into
a large jug. Stir well to mix.
Just before serving, stir in the
lemonade. Pour into glasses
containing crushed ice
and decorate with a blackberry
and mint sprig.

Serves 20

Limeade

6 limes
125 g (4 oz) caster sugar
750 ml (1¼ pints) boiling
    water
pinch of salt
ice cubes

to decorate
lime wedges
mint leaves

Halve the limes then squeeze the juice into a large jug. Put the squeezed lime halves into a heatproof jug with the sugar and boiling water and leave to infuse for 15 minutes. Add the salt, give the infusion a good stir, then strain it into the jug with the lime juice. Add half a dozen ice cubes, cover and refrigerate for 2 hours or until chilled. To serve, place 3–4 ice cubes in each glass and pour the limeade over them. Add a lime wedge and a mint leaf to decorate.

Serves 8

Lemonade on the Rocks

2 lemons, roughly
    chopped
2–3 tablespoons icing
    sugar
600 ml (1 pint) water
soda water or mineral
    water
ice cubes
lemon or lime slices, to
    decorate (optional)

Put the lemons, 2 tablespoons of the icing sugar and half the water in a food processor and process for a few seconds. Add the remaining water and process again. Taste and add more icing sugar if required; process briefly. Strain into 4 tumblers over ice and top up with soda or mineral water. Decorate with lemon or lime slices, if liked.

Serves 4

Midsummer Punch

125 g (4 oz) sugar
300 ml (½ pint) water
300 ml (½ pint) orange juice
300 ml (½ pint) pineapple juice
600 ml (1 pint) cold weak tea, strained
orange, lemon, apple and pineapple slices
crushed ice
300 ml (½ pint) ginger ale
mint sprigs, to decorate

Put the sugar and water into a saucepan and stir over a low heat until the sugar has dissolved. Leave to cool, then pour into a large jug or bowl. Stir in the fruit juices and cold tea, then add the sliced fruit and the crushed ice. To serve, pour into tall glasses and top up with ginger ale. Decorate with mint sprigs.

Serves 8–10

Bitter Sweet

crushed ice
600 ml (1 pint) sparkling
    mineral water
8 dashes Angostura
    bitters
handful of mint leaves
lemon or lime slices,
    to decorate

Put the crushed ice into a cocktail shaker, pour over 3 tablespoons of the mineral water and the bitters and add the mint leaves. Shake until a frost forms on the outside of the shaker. Pour into chilled glasses, top up with the remaining mineral water and decorate each glass with lemon or lime slices.

Serves 4

Grapefruit Mint Cooler

125 g (4 oz) sugar
125 ml (4 fl oz) water
handful of mint sprigs
juice of 4 large lemons
450 ml (¾ pint) grapefruit
    juice
crushed ice
250 ml (8 fl oz) soda
    water
mint sprigs, to decorate

Put the sugar and water into a heavy-based saucepan and stir over a low heat until dissolved. Leave to cool. Crush the mint leaves and stir them into the syrup. Cover and leave to stand for about 12 hours, then strain into a jug. Add the lemon and grapefruit juices to the strained syrup and stir well. Fill 6 old-fashioned glasses or tumblers with crushed ice and pour the cocktail into the glasses. Pour in the soda water and decorate with mint sprigs.

Serves 6

Variation

To make a Cranberry Mint Cooler, substitute cranberry juice for the grapefruit juice.

Alcohol-free Sangria

1 litre (1¾ pints) orange
    juice
sugar syrup (see page 7)
2 litres (3½ pints) red
    grape juice
juice of 6 lemons
juice of 6 limes
20–30 ice cubes
orange, lemon and lime
    slices, to decorate

Pour the orange juice and sugar
syrup, to taste, into a punch bowl
and stir. Add the grape, lemon
and lime juices and stir
thoroughly to mix. Add the ice,
then float the fruit slices on top.

Serves 20

Warbine Cooler

2 dashes Angostura
    bitters
1 dash lime juice
ginger beer
lime slices, to decorate

Stir the bitters and lime juice together in a large wine glass. Top up with ginger beer and decorate with lime slices. Serve with a straw. Make to order at a party.

Serves 1

Clayton's Pussyfoot

½ measure lemon syrup
½ measure orange juice
1 measure cola
3 cracked ice cubes

This cocktail is so quick and simple to make that it can be made to order at a party, making the drivers feel as welcome as the drinkers.

Put all the ingredients into a cocktail shaker and shake well. Strain into a cocktail glass.

Serves 1

Iced Mint Tea

12 mint sprigs
1 lemon, finely chopped
1 tablespoon sugar
1.2 litres (2 pints) weak
    tea, strained
ice cubes
lemon slices, to decorate

Chop up the mint sprigs and put them into a large heatproof jug with the lemon and sugar. Pour the tea into the jug and set the mixture aside to infuse for 20–30 minutes. Strain into another jug and chill in the refrigerator until required. To serve, pour into tumblers or tall glasses filled with ice and decorate each glass with lemon slices.

Serves 4

Fruit Punch

600 ml (1 pint) orange
  juice
600 ml (1 pint) apple
  juice
150 ml (¼ pint) water
½ teaspoon ground
  ginger
½ teaspoon mixed spice
brown sugar (optional)
1 apple, thinly sliced,
  to decorate

A delicious warm, alcohol-free punch that is ideal for autumn and winter parties.

Place the orange and apple juices, water and spices in a saucepan and bring gently to the boil, adding sugar to taste if required. Simmer the mixture for 5 minutes. Pour the punch into a warmed bowl and float the apple slices on top.

Serves 6

Cranberry Crush

crushed ice
1.8 litres (3 pints)
    cranberry juice
600 ml (1 pint) orange
    juice
600 ml (1 pint) ginger ale
orange and lemon
    wedges, to decorate

Half-fill a large punch bowl with crushed ice. Pour in the cranberry and orange juices and stir to mix. Top up with the ginger ale and decorate with orange and lemon wedges. Serve immediately.

Serves 15

Tip

For a special occasion, float red rose petals on top of the punch.

Tropical Treat

900 ml (1½ pints) natural
    yogurt
1 large ripe pineapple,
    peeled and roughly
    chopped
300 ml (½ pint) sparkling
    mineral water
ice cubes
sugar syrup (see page 7)
mint sprigs, to decorate

Place the yogurt, pineapple and
mineral water in a food processor
and process until smooth, in
batches if necessary. Put the ice
cubes into a tall jug, then pour in
the drink through a very fine
strainer. Stir, then add sugar
syrup to taste and stir again. Pour
into tall glasses and decorate
with mint sprigs.

Serves 4

Nursery Fizz

crushed ice
orange juice
ginger ale

to decorate
cocktail cherry
orange slice

Fill a large wine glass with crushed ice and pour in equal measures of orange juice and ginger ale. Decorate with a cocktail cherry and an orange slice speared on to a cocktail stick. Serve with a straw. Make to order at a party.

Serves 1

Green Devil

juice of 5–6 limes,
    strained
1.2 litres (2 pints)
    sparkling mineral
    water
1 teaspoon Angostura
    bitters
12 ice cubes

Combine all the ingredients,
except the ice cubes, in a jug and
stir together. Divide the ice cubes
among 4 tall glasses then pour in
the drink.

Serves 4

Spiced Ginger Punch

2 oranges
cloves, to taste
1 cm (½ inch) piece of
    fresh root ginger,
    peeled and grated
2 litres (3½ pints) ginger
    ale
10 cm (4 inches)
    cinnamon stick

Stud the oranges with the cloves, then bake them in a preheated oven at 180ºC (350ºF), Gas Mark 4 for about 25 minutes, until they are a rich golden colour. Cut the oranges into slices using a sharp knife then put them into a saucepan with the grated ginger, ginger ale and the cinnamon stick. Bring steadily to boiling point, but do not boil. Remove the cinnamon stick then pour the punch into heatproof glasses and serve.

Serves 12

Prohibition Punch

125 ml (4 fl oz) sugar
  syrup (see page 7)
350 ml (12 fl oz) lemon
  juice
900 ml (1½ pints) apple
  juice
ice cubes
2.5 litres (4 pints) ginger
  ale
orange slices,
  to decorate

Stir together the sugar syrup, lemon and apple juices in a large chilled jug. Add the ice cubes and pour in the ginger ale. Decorate with orange slices and serve.

Serves 25–30

Fruit and Vegetables

Anita

Brown Horny Toad

Tenderberry

Caribbean Cocktail

River Cruise

San Francisco

Banana Shake

Bugs Bunny

Romanov Fizz

Carrot Cream

Coco-oco

Tomato and Cucumber Cooler

Guavarama

Cranberry, Raspberry and
    Orange Crush

Appleade

Carib Cream

Frosty Lime

Parson's Special

Apple Eye

Peach, Pear and Raspberry
    Crush

Anita

3 ice cubes
1 measure orange juice
1 measure lemon juice
3 dashes Angostura
    bitters
soda water

to decorate
lemon slice
orange slice

Put the ice cubes into a cocktail shaker with the orange and lemon juices and bitters and shake well. Strain into a tumbler and top up with soda water. Decorate with lemon and orange slices.

Serves 1

Brown Horny Toad

4–5 crushed ice cubes
2 measures pineapple
    juice
2 measures orange juice
1 measure lemon juice
1 tablespoon grenadine
1 teaspoon sugar syrup
    (see page 7)
pinch of ground cinnamon
pinch of ground cloves

to decorate
orange slice
lemon slice

Put the ice cubes into a cocktail shaker. Pour in the pineapple, orange and lemon juices, and the grenadine and add the sugar syrup and spices. Shake until a frost forms on the outside of the shaker. Strain into a highball glass and decorate with orange and lemon slices.

Serves 1

Variation

To make a Green Horny Toad, substitute lime juice for the orange juice and use lime syrup instead of the grenadine.

Tenderberry

6–8 strawberries
1 measure grenadine
1 measure double cream
crushed ice
1 measure ginger ale
ground ginger
strawberry, to decorate
     (optional)

Place the strawberries, grenadine and cream in a food processor with some crushed ice and process for 30 seconds. Pour into a glass. Add the ginger ale and stir. Sprinkle a little ground ginger on top and decorate with a strawberry, if liked.

Serves 1

Variation

Raspberries make a delicious alternative in this recipe, but it is best to strain the drink after blending to remove the pips.

Caribbean Cocktail

1 mango, peeled and
     stoned
1 banana
juice of 1 large orange
1 dash lime juice
8–10 ice cubes
lime slices, to decorate

Put the mango, banana, orange
and lime juices in a food
processor and process until
smooth. Put the ice into
2 highball glasses and pour the
cocktail over it. Decorate with
lime slices.

Serves 2

River Cruise

500 g (1 lb) cantaloupe
    melon flesh
grated rind and juice of
    2 lemons
2 tablespoons sugar
600 ml (1 pint) chilled
    soda water

Remove and discard any melon seeds. Put the flesh into a food processor and process to a smooth purée. Scrape the purée into a large jug. Put the lemon rind and juice into a small saucepan with the sugar and stir over a low heat until the sugar has dissolved. Strain the lemon mixture into the melon purée and mix well. Chill in the refrigerator. Stir in the chilled soda water just before serving.

Serves 4–6

Variation

If you have a juicer, put the melon flesh through it to make a delicious clear juice to use in this drink instead of the melon purée.

San Francisco

3 ice cubes

1 measure orange juice

1 measure lemon juice

1 measure pineapple
   juice

1 measure grapefruit
   juice

2 dashes grenadine

1 egg white

soda water

to decorate

lemon slice

lime slice

cocktail cherry

orange spiral

Put the ice cubes into a cocktail shaker and pour in the orange, lemon, pineapple and grapefruit juices, grenadine and egg white. Shake well then strain into a large goblet. Top up with soda water and decorate with the lemon and lime slices, a cocktail cherry on a cocktail stick and an orange spiral. Serve with a straw.

Serves 1

Banana Shake

1 ripe banana, chopped
juice of 1 orange
1 teaspoon honey
300 ml (½ pint) full-fat
    milk
8 ice cubes
ground cinnamon

Place the banana, orange juice, honey and milk in a food processor and process until smooth. Pour over ice into 2 tall glasses and sprinkle with cinnamon.

Serves 2

Variation

To make a Mango Shake, substitute a ripe mango for the banana. Peel the mango and remove the stone before processing. You may wish to leave out the honey if the mango is very sweet.

Bugs Bunny

50 ml (2 fl oz) carrot juice
50 ml (2 fl oz) orange
    juice
4–6 ice cubes
1 dash Tabasco sauce
1 celery stick, to
    decorate

Pour the carrot and orange juices
into a tumbler over ice, add a
dash of Tabasco and decorate
with a celery stick.

Serves 1

Romanov Fizz

8–10 ripe strawberries,
 hulled
125 ml (4 fl oz) orange
 juice
2 ice cubes
125 ml (4 fl oz) soda
 water

Put the strawberries and orange juice into a food processor and process until smooth. Place 1 ice cube in each of 2 sour glasses or wine glasses and add the strawberry liquid. Pour the soda water into the food processor, process briefly and use to top up the glasses. Stir briskly, and serve.

Serves 2

Carrot Cream

250 ml (8 fl oz) carrot
    juice
300 ml (½ pint) single
    cream
4 egg yolks
125 ml (4 fl oz) orange
    juice
20 ice cubes
orange slices, to
    decorate

Put the carrot juice, cream, egg yolks and orange juice into a cocktail shaker and shake well. Divide the ice cubes among 4 tall glasses and pour the carrot drink on top. Decorate with orange slices and serve immediately. Serve with straws.

Serves 4

Coco-oco

crushed ice
4 teaspoons creamed
    coconut or coconut
    syrup
2 teaspoons lemon juice
1 teaspoon maraschino
    syrup
100 ml (3½ fl oz) full-fat
    milk
4 dashes Angostura
    bitters

to decorate
pineapple leaf
pineapple wedge
cocktail cherry

Put the ice into a food processor and add the creamed coconut or coconut syrup, lemon juice, maraschino syrup, milk and bitters. Process for a few seconds. Pour into a tall glass and decorate with a pineapple leaf, a pineapple wedge and a cocktail cherry. Serve with a straw.

Serves 1

fruit and vegetables

Tomato and Cucumber Cooler

crushed ice
150 ml (¼ pint) tomato
    juice
25 g (1 oz) cucumber,
    peeled
2 dashes lemon juice
2 dashes Worcestershire
    sauce
salt and pepper
cucumber slice, to
    decorate

Put a little crushed ice into a food processor. Add the tomato juice, cucumber, lemon juice, Worcestershire sauce and salt and pepper to taste and process well. Pour the drink into a cocktail glass and decorate with a cucumber slice.

Serves 1

Guavarama

crushed ice
200 ml (7 fl oz) guava
    juice
2 teaspoons lime juice
4 teaspoons blackcurrant
    syrup
5 dashes rum essence
melon slice, to decorate

Put some crushed ice into a food processor and add the guava juice, lime juice, blackcurrant syrup and rum essence. Process thoroughly then strain into a chilled cocktail glass and decorate with a melon slice.

Serves 1

Cranberry, Raspberry and Orange Crush

200 ml (7 fl oz) cranberry juice
100 ml (3½ fl oz) orange juice
250 ml (8 oz) raspberries
3 scoops orange sorbet, plus extra to decorate
sugar syrup (see page 7) (optional)

Put the cranberry juice, orange juice, raspberries and sorbet into a food processor and process until frothy. Taste and add sugar syrup, if required. Serve in cocktail glasses, each with an extra scoop of sorbet.

Serves 2–3

Appleade

2 large dessert apples
600 ml (1 pint) boiling
    water
½ teaspoon sugar
ice cubes
apple slices, to decorate

Chop the apples and place in a bowl. Pour the boiling water over the apples and add the sugar. Leave to stand for 10 minutes, then strain into a jug and allow to cool. Pour over ice cubes in tall glasses and decorate with apple slices. Serve with straws.

Serves 3

Carib Cream

1 small banana, chopped
1 measure lemon juice
1 measure full-fat milk
crushed ice
1 teaspoon finely
  chopped walnuts

Place the banana, lemon juice
and milk in a food processor with
some crushed ice and process on
maximum speed until smooth.
Pour into a cocktail glass and
sprinkle the chopped walnuts
on top just before serving.

Serves 1

Frosty Lime

1 scoop lime sorbet
1 measure grapefruit
   juice
4 teaspoons mint syrup

to decorate
mint strips
lemon slices

Put the sorbet, grapefruit juice and syrup into a food processor and process on high speed for about 30 seconds. Strain into a Champagne glass and decorate with mint strips and lemon slices.

Serves 1

Parson's Special

4 dashes grenadine
120 ml (4 fl oz) orange
    juice
1 egg yolk
3 ice cubes

Put all the ingredients into a
cocktail shaker and shake well.
Stain into a tumbler.

Serves 1

Apple Eye

2 measures apple juice
½ measure blackcurrant
    syrup
1 measure double cream
crushed ice
ground cinnamon
apple slices, to decorate

Place the apple juice,
blackcurrant syrup and cream
in a food processor with
some crushed ice. Process on
maximum speed for 30 seconds.
Pour into a cocktail glass and
sprinkle a little cinnamon on top.
Decorate with apple slices.

Serves 1

fruit and vegetables

Peach, Pear and Raspberry Crush

1 ripe peach, skinned, stoned and chopped
1 ripe pear, peeled, cored and chopped
125 g (4 oz) raspberries
200 ml (7 fl oz) peach juice
crushed ice
pear slices, to decorate

Put the peach, pear, raspberries and peach juice into a food processor with some ice and process until smooth. Serve in cocktail glasses and decorate with pear slices.

Serves 2–3

Round the Clock

Café Astoria

Chocolate Shake

Egg Nog

Tutti Frutti Verbena Cocktail

Florentine Coffee

Iced Apple Tea

Catherine Blossom

Limey

Virgin Colada

St Clements

Jersey Lily

Grenadine Soda

Pink Tonic

Shirley Temple

Honeymoon

Cinderella

Keep Sober

Virgin Mary

Dandy

Orange and Papaya Fizz

Nairobi Night

Café Astoria

1½ measures coffee
   essence
2 measures full-fat milk
1 measure pineapple
   juice
½ measure lemon juice
3 ice cubes, crushed
chocolate shavings, to
   decorate

A great drink to start the day, or to end a party in the early hours.

Place the coffee essence, milk, pineapple juice and lemon juice in a food processor with the ice and process on maximum speed for 30 seconds. Pour into a cocktail glass and sprinkle the chocolate shavings on top just before serving.

Serves 1

Chocolate Shake

2 measures chocolate
  syrup
2 scoops chocolate ice
  cream
1 scoop vanilla ice cream
250 ml (8 fl oz) full-fat
  milk
whipped cream, to
  decorate (optional)

Pour all of the ingredients into
a food processor. Process well
until the desired thickness is
reached. Pour into a tall glass.
Decorate with whipped cream, if
liked, and serve with a straw.

Serves 1

Egg Nog

1 egg
sugar syrup (see page 7)
250 ml (8 fl oz) full-fat
    milk
cracked ice
grated nutmeg, to
    decorate

Combine the egg, sugar syrup to taste, milk and ice in a cocktail shaker and shake well. Strain into a large goblet and sprinkle with grated nutmeg.

Serves 1

Tutti Frutti Verbena Cocktail

3 sachets verbena tea
600 ml (1 pint) boiling
    water
juice of 2 oranges
juice of 2 lemons
150 ml (¼ pint) apricot
    juice
150 ml (¼ pint) pineapple
    juice
ice cubes

Put the sachets of verbena tea into a heatproof jug, pour over the boiling water and leave to infuse. When the tea is cold, remove the sachets from the jug. Pour the tea into another jug and add the juice from the oranges and lemons, the apricot juice, pineapple juice and a few ice cubes.

Serves 4–6

Variation

Try different flavours of fruit tea, such as elderflower, rosehip or cranberry in place of the verbena tea.

Florentine Coffee

espresso coffee
1 drop almond essence
1 sugar cube (optional)

Pour the coffee into a warmed cup or heatproof glass. Add the almond essence and sugar, if using, and stir.

Serves 1

Iced Apple Tea

¾ pint chilled weak tea
450 ml (¾ pint) apple
    juice
juice of 1 lemon
1 teaspoon sugar
    (optional)
ice cubes

to decorate
lemon slices
orange slices
mint sprigs

Mix the tea with the apple juice,
lemon juice and sugar, if using.
Add plenty of ice and decorate
with the lemon and orange
slices and mint sprigs. Serve
in tumblers or tea glasses.

Serves 6–8

Catherine Blossom

200 ml (7 fl oz) orange
    juice
2 teaspoons maple syrup
2 scoops orange sorbet
soda water

Put the orange juice, maple
syrup and orange sorbet into a
food processor and process for
15 seconds. Pour into a tall glass
and top up with soda water.

Serves 1

Limey

1 measure lime juice
½ measure lemon juice
½ egg white
3 cracked ice cubes
cocktail cherry, to
    decorate

This makes a refreshing late afternoon drink for a warm summer's day.

Put the lime and lemon juces, egg white and ice cubes into a cocktail shaker and shake well. Strain into a cocktail glass and decorate with a cocktail cherry on a cocktail stick.

Serves 1

Virgin Colada

1 measure coconut
cream
2 measures pineapple
juice
crushed ice
pineapple wedge, to
decorate

Place the coconut cream, pineapple juice and crushed ice into a food processor and process, or shake in a cocktail shaker. Pour into a tall glass and decorate with a pineapple wedge. Serve with a straw.

Serves 1

St Clements

2 measures orange juice
2 measures bitter lemon
4 ice cubes
orange slice, to decorate

Pour the orange juice and bitter lemon over ice in a tumbler, stir together and decorate with the orange slice.

Serves 1

Jersey Lily

150 ml (¼ pint) sparkling
    apple juice
2 dashes Angostura
    bitters
¼ teaspoon caster sugar
ice cubes
cocktail cherry, to
    decorate

Put the apple juice, bitters, sugar
and ice cubes in a cocktail
shaker. Shake well, then strain
into a wine glass. Decorate with
a cocktail cherry.

Serves 1

Variation

Sparkling grape juice,
either red or white,
makes a refreshing
substitute for the
apple juice.

Grenadine Soda

1 scoop orange sorbet
1 scoop raspberry sorbet
3 tablespoons grenadine
juice of 1 lime
2 scoops vanilla ice
    cream
250 ml (8 fl oz) soda
    water

to decorate
1 finely chopped orange
    slice
raspberries

Put the sorbets, grenadine and lime juice into a food processor and process until slushy. Pour into glasses and put the vanilla ice cream on top. Top up with soda water. Stir gently, and decorate with the fruit. Serve with straws.

Serves 2

Pink Tonic

2–3 dashes Angostura
    bitters
4–6 ice cubes
250 ml (8 fl oz) tonic
    water
lime wedge, to decorate

Drop the bitters over ice in a
tumbler, add the tonic water
and stir well. Decorate with a
lime wedge.

Serves 1

Shirley Temple

4–5 ice cubes
1 dash grenadine
ginger ale
2 cocktail cherries,
  to decorate

Put the ice cubes in a glass. Add the grenadine and top up with the ginger ale. Decorate with 2 cherries on a cocktail stick.

Serves 1

Honeymoon

crushed ice
1 measure maple syrup
   or clear honey
4 teaspoons lime juice
1 measure orange juice
1 measure apple juice
cocktail cherry,
   to decorate

Put some crushed ice into a cocktail shaker and add the maple syrup or honey, lime juice, orange juice and apple juice. Shake well then strain into a chilled cocktail glass. Decorate with a cherry on a cocktail stick.

Serves 1

Cinderella

1 measure lemon juice
1 measure pineapple
    juice
1 measure orange juice
1 dash grenadine
3 ice cubes, cracked
soda water
pineapple slices,
    to decorate

Put the lemon, pineapple and orange juices, grenadine and ice into a cocktail shaker and shake well. Strain into a tall tumbler. Top up with soda water and decorate with pineapple slices. Serve with a straw.

Serves 1

Keep Sober

½ measure grenadine
½ measure lemon syrup
3 measures tonic water
soda water
ice cubes (optional)

Put the grenadine, lemon syrup and tonic water in a tumbler and stir together. Top up with soda water and add ice cubes, if liked.

Serves 1

Variation

For a tangier drink, replace the grenadine with lime syrup and decorate the drink with lime slices.

Virgin Mary

4 measures tomato juice
ice cubes
½ measure lemon juice
2 dashes Worcestershire
    sauce
1 dash Tabasco sauce
celery stick, to decorate

Pour the tomato juice into a glass
over ice cubes, add the lemon
juice and Worcestershire and
Tabasco sauces and stir well.
Serve with a celery stick.

Serves 1

Variation

For special occasions,
dip the rim of the glass
into beaten egg white,
then into celery salt
for an attractive and
tasty frosting.

Dandy

3 measures apple juice
1 measure strawberry
    syrup
1 measure lime juice
10 blackberries

to decorate
blackberry
mint sprig

Put the apple juice, strawberry syrup, lime juice and blackberries in a food processor with some cracked ice and process until smooth. Pour into a tall glass. Decorate with a blackberry and a mint sprig.

Serves 1

Orange and Papaya Fizz

1 papaya, peeled,
   quartered and
   deseeded
250 ml (8 fl oz) orange
   juice
4–6 ice cubes
sparkling mineral water
mint sprigs, to decorate

Place the papaya and orange juice
in a food processor and process
for about 30 seconds, or until
smooth. Put 2–3 ice cubes into 2
tall glasses, pour in the drink and
top up with the sparkling mineral
water. Stir and serve, decorated
with mint sprigs.

Serves 2

Nairobi Night

450 ml (¾ pint) freshly
    made coffee
caster sugar
4 tablespoons single
    cream
150 ml (¼ pint) vanilla ice
    cream
4 ice cubes
drinking chocolate
    powder, to decorate

Pour the coffee into a bowl and
stir in sugar to taste. Set aside to
cool. Whisk together the cream
and ice cream, then beat into the
coffee. Continue beating until
smooth and frothy. Pour into a
jug and chill in the refrigerator
for 1 hour, stirring occasionally.
To serve, pour into 2 large
goblets and float the ice cubes
on top. Sprinkle with drinking
chocolate powder to decorate.

Serves 2